Money Matters

Workbook

ISBN-13:   978-1466394094

ISBN-10:   1466394099

BISAC: EDU013000

            Education / Finance

Contents

Introduction

There are two things needed these days: First, for rich people to find out how poor people live; and second, for poor people to find out how rich people work.

- John Foster

Reading *Money Matters* and the *Money Matters Devotional* is a great first step, but without putting it into action it will always remain head knowledge. Knowledge is only one part of getting to the place of financial freedom. Even though we have learned all the Scriptures and have renewed our mind and started sowing, etc we still have our part to do. God is not going to come down from heaven and suddenly make everything OK. We need to be wise stewards and faithful with the little that we have too, so He can add to it.[1]

I firmly believe that if God wanted us only to depend on Him and not also use our common sense, then He wouldn't have given us a brain! We do have a brain and we have to use it as best we can and trust God in all that we do at the same time. I hope that's not too harsh but seriously Christians, let's stop being wimps and stand up and take the dominion that God has given us and use it. This section is the practical, common sense section of *Money Matters* that will help you take control of your finances and put them in order. I'm sure that when God sees that you are ready to handle more, then He will give you more.

Our lives are carefully planned out by God. He doesn't just take it as it comes and hope for the best. He has carefully mapped out our lives, as He clearly says in Jeremiah 1,

---

[1] Matthew 25:14-30

"before you were in your mother's womb I already knew you".[2] Again, later on in Jeremiah, God says clearly that He has a plan and purpose for your life.[3] He has a blueprint for each and every one of our lives. We were also moulded in His image and made like Him. With all this evidence it stands to reason that we should also be careful planners. The quote above by John Foster is profound because it gives us a key. Why do the rich become richer and the poor become poorer? Is it because the rich have a plan and a purpose and the poor just live in defeat? Some poor people do become rich, don't they? Ask them how. Most of them say that they were determined and many of them say that they had plans and goals.

Points to ponder:

You cannot force God and you cannot force the world's system. Obedience to God is essential and obedience to the worlds system is just as essential if we want success in our personal finances.

"Let every soul be subject to the governing authorities. For there is no authority except from God, and the authorities that exist are appointed by God. Therefore whoever resists the authority resists the ordinance of God, and those who resist will bring judgment on themselves."

- Romans 13:1-2

Asking God to guide you when working out your monthly budget is the best thing you could do. Invite God to join you and to be a part of your planning. He alone knows what the future holds and what you need to do to get the best out of your life and out of your finances. Start in Malachi 3:8-12, as this is the only place in the Bible where God dares you,

---

[2] Jeremiah 1:5
[3] Jeremiah 29:11

where he challenges you to test Him. The promise He gives you is great and it is His word, assuring you of what He will do for you.

Seed sown into the ground needs watering, weeding and caring for and this is because the harvest is not immediate. The crop must mature and it is too easy to lose motivation and to stop believing that it will work while we wait. Waiting will require a great deal of discipline. The most important thing to understand is that you won't always have instant results and that it is not going to be easy. In 1991 I discovered Matthew 6:25-34, a section of the Bible where God says that we should not worry and trust Him to take care of us. It became very real to me and was something that I tried to live by.

Success came for the first time in 2000, nine years later. Practice makes perfect and I did my best to apply this principle in my life, having a measure of success at times. My goal was to live in the freedom of not worrying. For nearly ten years, after failing many times and then getting up again and repeating this cycle over and over again, I finally managed to live worry free. Faith is a continuing process and I don't think you ever get it completely mastered but you do get very close.

A budget is not an evil thing, it doesn't mean you don't trust God to care for you – it's a wise tool to manage money! Blind faith never will produce anything. Your budget is the starting point for your faith to be put into action. How will you ever know how much He has provided if you have no record of it and no way to prove it? My budget is evidence of God's provision!

Over the years I have seen so many people not enjoying life to the full because their financial situation is limiting them. It really doesn't need to be this way. In spending time with people in various financial situations I realised that most of the time they end up having their money control them simply because they don't know **how** to control their money. There are many great books on money and all kind of ideas and suggestions on how to make money and do all kinds of things with money, but how does that help the average person who is simply trying to start managing what they have? This workbook is a practical tool that will help you get started at step one. Once you've achieved everything suggested in this book then go ahead to the next step and read other books that provide more complex advice about your money.

Money does matter because if you are not in control of your money then your money will control you. My desire is that if you are in a position where your money is controlling you, that you will take back the reigns and be in control again. I do hope that this book will help you get back to the place where you are in control of your money and can live free from the constant worry money often brings.

So without further ado, get out your pencil, paper, calculator and eraser. Take a deep breath and promise not to fight with your husband/wife, children or dog while tackling this task.

Spreadsheets

The spreadsheets mentioned throughout this workbook are at the end of the book in the spreadsheets section.

Electronic Resources

For your convenience I have also created a website where you can download electronic spreadsheets. Go to www.d7church.co.uk/money.html

Step 1 Taking Control

Debt is not the end of the world, but if you don't deal with it, it could be the end of your world. So you have just slipped up financially, it's great that you recognise that and it is fantastic that you want to change your situation. However, the problem will not go away if you ignore it – it will definitely get worse and if you keep doing the same things you will keep getting the same results. The good news is that by taking control of the situation you will start to feel better immediately. By being sensible, you can turn the corner, so breathe a sigh of relief and give yourself a pat on the back for taking the first step towards financial freedom!

Managing your money is not about trying to increase your income to solve your financial problems. If you don't learn how to manage your expenses, no matter how much you earn, your expenses will always match or exceed your increase in income. For example, you get a nice pay rise and then because you feel so good about it, you go out and buy something expensive that you couldn't afford before. In time you will realize that the repayments are eating up the pay rise and you are left worse off. Wouldn't it have been better to save a huge portion of the pay rise in order to buy the things that you want for cash? Most people don't think that way – they are impatient and want everything instantly - but it makes more sense doesn't it?

If you have identified that your money is controlling you, causing you worry and distress, then the very first thing to do is to take control again – whether you are rich or poor, you need to take control. The way to do this is to assess where you are at financially and then formulate a plan to move forward from the position you are in now to the position you would like to be in. This process will take about four to six months if you want to do a thorough and proper job. But what is four to six months compared to the rest of your life? It is worth it isn't it?

So let us begin taking control by getting a good understanding of your current financial situation. In the spreadsheet section at the end of the work book you will see the first four spreadsheets (figures 1, 2, 3 & 4). These spreadsheets will help you begin to understand your current financial situation. The aim of these spreadsheets is to help you record everything that you spend your money on.

Before you even begin tackling the spreadsheets, admit that you are not in control of your money and make a commitment to gain control. This is the most important step of all because if you don't admit this to yourself, and perhaps even someone else if you want to be accountable, then you will end up living in denial and the habit will only get worse as time goes by.

1 - Collect all your bank statements, bills, receipts, payslips, etc.

You are going to find out how much you earn, spend and owe – and then work out how to keep in control of your money.   It's imperative that you record absolutely everything – every single penny. The most useful way of remembering what you spend your money on is to ask for a receipt for each and every one of your purchases. Where there is no way of getting a receipt or if you forget to ask for one, write the purchase detail and amount in a little note book.

2 – Record every penny into your spreadsheet.

Write down all your income and expenses in the appropriate columns in the spreadsheets provided (figures 1, 2, 3 & 4). The most effective way to start is to start from the first day of a month and record everything until the last day of the month. Do this for three months so that you can collect enough data to make a reasonable assessment of your situation.

Income	Other Income	Bills	Clothes	Debt	Education	Fitness & Leisure	Food	Gifts	Medical	Other	Phone	Rent	Savings	Charity	Travel
£1,450	£135	£226	£62	£125	£16	£39	£203	£10	£4	£53	£35	£750	£20	£4	£59
£200	£110	£52	£4	£25	£6	£39	£2	£10	£4	£2	£13	£750	£20	£4	£4
£200	£25	£11	£6	£100	£2		£65			£6	£12				£6
£450		£145	£18		£8		£3			£45	£10				£4
£600		£18	£2				£9								£4
			£3				£5								£4
			£10				£3								£4
			£19				£4								£2
							£8								£8
							£9								£5
							£60								£4
							£5								£4
							£8								£3
							£4								£2
							£6								£2
							£5								£2
							£7								

Figure 1 – Example

Figure 2- Month 1 ....

Fill in these sheets or download at www.moneymattersbook.co.uk

Figure 4- Month 3 ....
Fill in these sheets or download at www.moneymattersschool.co.uk

Recording Income and Expenses

Figure 1

This spreadsheet is an example.

Column 1 contains example headings of areas that money is spent on.

Column 2 is where the total is recorded and the remaining columns show the expenses of the particular month.

Figure 2, 3 & 4

These spreadsheets are blank and all you need to do is fill them in.

Decide what areas you most often spend money in and fill them in on the top grey row. For little bits and bobs that don't warrant an entire column use the column with the heading 'Other'.

Suggested Headings

Income

Use this heading to record your set salary and other definite monthly income not including overtime, savings, interest, etc. Record your full salary before Tax and NI is deducted.

Other Income

Use this heading to record any other income that you may get that varies from month to month e.g. overtime, dividends, and income from shares, etc.

* Don't count cash drawn from credit cards or loans, re-mortgages, etc as income – this is debt and once you start using the spreadsheets, you should be sure not to create more debt by obtaining cash from your credit card to cover your needs.

Bills

This heading should include your water, gas, electricity and council tax. If you would like to monitor these expenses in detail give each one a separate heading.

Charity

What you sow you reap, you may wish to have a heading that allows you to give generously to others and to your local church.

Clothes

Use this heading to record any clothes and cosmetics that you buy.

Optional - Don't use this column for children's school uniform as this can go under education.

Debt

If you have debt that is not settled, put it all into this column, that way you can see when it goes down and track it. Once you have settled your debt, take this heading out and don't allow for any more to incur.

Deductions/Bank Charges

Your tax, national insurance, bank charges and other deductions can go under this heading if you prefer to record your full salary before deductions under "Income".

Education

This column can be used for your children's education or any study that you may be doing or educational materials that you purchase regularly.

Household

Use for household items such as maintenance, carpet cleaning, garden items etc.

Fitness & Leisure

This heading can be used for gym membership, children's ballet classes, horse riding, golf, cinema, bowling, etc. Use this for anything along the lines of fitness and leisure. Even if you are on a tight budget, in fact especially if you are a tight budget this heading is important, as you can't live under continual financial pressure without letting off some steam every now and then.

If you plan the amount you are willing to spend in this area then you are less likely to indulge in impulse spending when things get a bit tough or when you find the routine and discipline of your budget a bit boring! We all need a break sometimes and we won't be effective in our money if we pull the purse strings too tight. Just remember, our money must work for us, not us working for our money.

Groceries

We all need to eat but even this heading can be managed wisely. This is a great place to save and simplify your life style but saving too much in this area could lead to poor health. Optional - If you eat at restaurants or buy takeaway meals regularly, have a separate heading for dining out, this way you can keep an eye on how much you actually spend in this area.

Dining Out

It is important to track small expenditures such as lunches and dining out. A little spent here and a little spent there does not seem like much but it adds up. If you don't track where you spend your money you won't be able to manage it.

Gifts

Birthdays, Christmas, children's parties, engagements, weddings, they happen all the time and they can get quite expensive so it's a good idea to keep track of how much you actually spend on gifts.

Medical

If you have medical insurance record the monthly cost under this heading. Also include pharmacy purchases, optometrist visits, dental visits, etc.

Other

This heading allows for little things that we don't need to dedicate an entire column to but they still need to be accounted for somewhere. It may be one hundred pounds or just ten or twenty pounds, it all depends on what your needs are. Things like developing a film, paying for stamps, etc.

Phone

This heading is self-explanatory; record all your phone and Internet costs here.

Rent/Mortgage

This heading is self-explanatory

Savings

Even if it's a few pennies in a piggy bank to start with or some small investments, it's always good to save.

Travel

If you are paying a car off then the repayments, maintenance and petrol will go under this heading. If you use the bus, train, tube or taxi service it should also goes here. You may like to separate petrol and other transport costs so that you can monitor your petrol consumption.

These headings are the most commonly used headings but each household has different requirements so choose headings that suit your household.

Step 1 Summary of What To Do Now:

- Decide on headings for your spreadsheet and fill them into the grey boxes on the top row of your spreadsheet.

- Start recording <u>all</u> your income and expenses on the spreadsheets under the relevant headings.

- At the end of each month total up your columns and place the totals under the headings.

- Start changing the way you spend your money even though we haven't yet put a plan in place. If there are things that you already notice that you are spending too much money on, cut down and try and discipline yourself in those areas.

- In the meantime keep reading on to the next chapters as you may want to apply some of the money saving or other ideas right away

Step 1 Notes:

Write down in the space below what you have noticed about your spending habits that you didn't know before and write down what you would like to do differently in future.

....

....

....

....

....

....

....

....

....

....

....

Step 2 Assessing The Situation

Well done, you have not only completed the first three months but also managed to take control of your money. By simply recording your income and expenditure you are already more in control of your money than you were before you started this exercise. You now have valuable information to work with. You are going to use this information to plan the way you are going to spend your money in future. Undoubtedly you will already see some frightening trends of where your money is going, perhaps things that you were never aware of before.

The next exercise is to assess the three months of data that you have gathered and to work out your average income and expenditure. Spreadsheets 5 & 6 will help you to work it out.

Figure 5 – Averages Example

	Income	Other Income	Bills	Clothes	Debt	Education	Fitness/Leisure	Food	Gifts	Medical	Other	Phone	Rent	Savings	Charity	Travel
Mth 1	£2,200	£111	£213	£40	£250	£65	£40	£320	£20	£50	£65	£65	£850	£20	£15	£93
Mth 2	£2,200	£150	£218	£85	£225	£23	£40	£350	£78	£14	£72	£83	£850	£20	£15	£93
Mth 3	£2,200	£168	£179	£32	£276	£67	£40	£295	£13	£55	£43	£71	£850	£20	£15	£93
Total	£6,600	£429	£610	£157	£751	£155	£120	£965	£111	£119	£180	£219	£2,550	£60	£45	£279
Divide	3	3	3	3	3	3	3	3	3	3	3	3	3	3	3	3
Ave	£2,200	£143	£203	£52	£250	£52	£40	£322	£37	£40	£60	£73	£850	£20	£15	£93

Figure 6 – Your Averages

	Income	Other Income	Bills	Clothes	Debt	Education	Fitness/Leisure	Food	Gifts	Medical	Other	Phone	Rent	Savings	Charity	Travel
Mth 1																
Mth 2																
Mth 3																
Total																
Divide	3	3	3	3	3	3	3	3	3	3	3	3	3	3	3	3
Ave																

Step 2 Summary of What To Do Now:

- Fill in the spreadsheet to calculate your average income and expenses. As per the example (figure 5), fill in the totals for each heading for months 1, 2 & 3 (the very left hand column shows the months).

- Once you've filled in each month, add them up and put the total for each heading in the total row.

- Take the total and divide by 3 to give you the average for each heading. These averages will help you realise exactly where your money is going and will help you plan how you intend to spend your money in future.

Step 2 Notes:

Write down in the space below which heading/s you would like to cut down your spending on and which heading/s cause you the most concern.

……

……

……

……

……

……

……

……

……

……

……

……

Step 3 Sorting Out Debt

Before we continue to plan how to better use your money, we need to take a look at debt. Most of the time debt is unnecessary and caused by a lack of discipline. Occasionally it is unforeseen circumstances and you have ended up in debt by things like car expenses, medical bills, etc. Debt, with the exception of a mortgage and perhaps your first new car, is very dangerous. The reason why debt is so dangerous is that when living beyond your means, you are effectively borrowing from your future self. By spending tomorrow's money today, all you are doing is making yourself broke in the future.

Are you a credit addict?

Do you recognise any of the following symptoms?

- Your credit-card company increases your credit limit by £1000. To celebrate, you buy a few treats to cheer yourself up.
- You panic or break out in a sweat when you see another bill on the doormat.
- You've buried your head in the sand and have stopped opening your bank, loan and credit card statements. You're a financial ostrich!
- You've started skipping payments: "I need a breather; I'll skip this month's repayment and make up the difference later."
- You see your credit-card limit as a *target,* not a *limit.*
- You see something that you can't afford, yet think: "No problem, I'll just stick it on my plastic."
- You don't have any idea where your money goes, how much you're spending or how much you owe.

- Talking or thinking about money makes you seriously stressed, so you avoid the subject – or lie awake at night worrying.

- Your money goes purely on meeting your interest payments so you don't chip away at your debt at all.

- You start thinking that those adverts for 'affordable secured loans', featuring 'celebrities', look like a good idea. You decide to borrow a little extra on top for a holiday – after all, you *need* one.

If these sound familiar, then you need to examine your spending and borrowing habits. If you display several of these symptoms, you may already be a credit junkie! Life in this day and age is fast and furious and there is a lot of pressure to "keep up with the Joneses". Most of us want what is out of our reach and we want it now, so we turn to credit.

Some Frightening Facts

If you have done a balance transfer to a new credit card for £2,000 (including a 9 months interest free period) and pay the minimum balance (2% of the monthly balance) each month, after 12 months you will still owe £1,739.42 and after 24 months you will owe £1,587.09.

To totally clear a credit card balance of £2,000 by making only the minimum payment each month it will take you 601 payments (or 50 years) to pay it off. The total interest that you would have paid in that time would be £3,858.91

Another way of looking at it is in the following table. This table shows how much interest you would pay if you were to pay the minimum balance of a £1,000 (15.9% APR) credit card each month (with no 9 months interest free period) and how many years it would take you to pay it off.

Year End	Balance	Interest Paid	Year End	Balance	Interest Paid
1	£1,856	£306	20	£396	£65
2	£1,712	£282	21	£365	£60
3	£1,578	£260	22	£337	£56
4	£1,455	£240	23	£311	£51
5	£1,341	£221	24	£286	£47
6	£1,236	£204	25	£264	£44
7	£1,140	£188	26	£243	£40
8	£1,051	£173	27	£224	£37
9	£969	£160	28	£207	£34
10	£893	£147	29	£191	£32
11	£824	£136	30	£176	£29
12	£759	£125	31	£162	£27
13	£700	£116	32	£149	£25
14	£645	£106	33	£138	£23
15	£595	£98	34	£127	£21
16	£549	£91	35	£117	£19
17	£506	£83	36	£108	£18
18	£466	£77	37	£100	£17
19	£430	£71	38	£92	£15

This table (below) shows how you can pay the same card off much quicker simply by paying 5% of your balance each month instead of 2%. By overpaying by a mere 3% you can clear your credit card in 12 years instead of 40 or more years and save £3,026.

Year End	Balance	Interest Paid	Year End	Balance	Interest Paid
1	£1,325	£261	7	£89	18
2	£845	£166	8	£57	11
3	£539	£106	9	£36	7
4	£344	£68	10	£23	5
5	£220	£43	11	£15	3
6	£140	£27.58	12	£9	2

The final table (below) shows that by paying 10% of your balance each month you can pay your credit card off in around 4 years, giving you a saving of £3,442.

Year End	Balance	Interest Paid	Year End	Balance	Interest Paid
1	£737	£203	3	£83	£23
2	£248	£68	4	£28	£8

Debt Consolidation

This is seldom the answer to managing your debt for these simple reasons:

1. It usually takes longer to pay off a consolidation loan which will make your interest higher.
2. You could lull yourself into a false sense of security because your monthly repayments are less than before. This could lead to you feeling OK to acquire a little more debt.

3. There are often financial penalties and charges to paying off a loan earlier that the agreed time. In some cases you are even required to pay the interest for the entire repayment period even if you pay the loan off earlier than the agreed time.

However, consolidation loans are typically at a lower rate than credit cards.

The bottom line is that the banks make money from you being indebted to them so they don't want you to pay off your loans sooner. In fact, they would rather encourage you to get deeper into debt so that their business gains more profit at your expense.

Interest Calculation on Credit Purchases

The next thing to do is to work out how much in interest you are paying on credit purchases. This will give you a clear picture of how much money you could be saving if you were debt free - do this as a deterrent against further credit and interest payments.

In the following spreadsheet (figure 7) write down three months worth of interest that you have paid on each of your bills in the interest column. Total up each set and place the total in the "Total" box then divide the total by three and place the answer in the "Average" box. Do this for all your debt and once you have completed the exercise, add up all the average boxes and write the total into the "Ave Monthly Interest Total" box. This will give you the average interest that you are paying each month.

I hope at this point you don't feel overwhelmed by all this paperwork? If you haven't been disciplined in your money at all then all this paperwork may seem a little daunting to you. Don't be put off, once you have got familiar with a system that works for you then it will simply form a routine in your life.

Month	To whom	Interest	Average
1			
2			
3			
Total			
1			
2			
3			
Total			
1			
2			
3			
Total			
1			
2			
3			
Total			
Ave Monthly Interest Total			

Figure 7 – Average Monthly Interest

Fill in these sheets or download at www. moneymattersbook.co.uk

Debt Summary – Monthly

Record all money that you owe (debt) in the boxes below, include obvious debt like credit cards, overdrafts, store cards, etc. Also include any other money that you owe like money borrowed from parents, etc. Transfer the average interest figures from the previous table that you did (figure 7) and fill in into the "Ave Interest" box in this table (figure 8). Arrange all your entries from the highest to the lowest average interest. If you own a car put that in second last and if you have a mortgage fill that it last so that your car and mortgage appears at the bottom of the box.

If you're serious about getting your money sorted out then start tackling the debt. The debt with the highest average interest is the one that should go first, pay all that you can into this debt then close this account and focus on the next debt on your list.

To whom	Balance Due	Monthly	Ave Interest
TOTAL	£	£	£

Figure 8 – Your Debt Summary

Fill in these sheets or download at www. moneymattersbook.co.uk

Start Saving On Interest Right Away

1. Stop spending on credit right away.

   Make a commitment and stick to it no matter what. The best thing to do is to cut up all your credit cards - that way you won't be able to spend when you're feeling a little down.

2. Put your savings into your debts.

   Use your savings to pay off your debts, starting with the highest average interest debt. It doesn't make sense to pay £200 a year in interest on a £1000 credit-card debt, while earning a measly £40 on £1000 of savings. All you're doing is losing £160 a year. You should put enough aside for emergencies, but use the bulk of your savings to pay off debt.

3. Do a balance transfer on your credit cards.

   Many credit card companies charge 0% interest for 6-10 months on balance transfers. Change credit card companies and use what you were spending on interest to help pay off the card faster. Just before your 0% introductory offer is up, apply for another 0% card and continue the process until your cards are all closed.

BEWARE:

Take into consideration any annual card fees while you are doing this. If you do not pay off the entire amount before the introductory offer is up, you could end up paying interest on the entire loan period and you could end up paying a higher interest rate than before you changed your credit card - research these things and read the fine print carefully!

Do not spend on the card that you've carried out a balance transfer to. The banks don't offer these great interest free periods just to be nice! Any purchases made with balance transfers are left to accumulate interest while you are paying off your balance transfer first. This means spending will stay on the card, quickly gathering interest but you can't start paying that off until the entire balance transfer debt has been paid in full. For loads of fantastic money savings ideas visit www.moneysavingexpert.com.

Negotiate

You will be amazed at what you can achieve if you simply inform your bank about your struggles and negotiate a better arrangement with them. For your convenience I have included some sample letters that you can use or download from www.d7church.co.uk/money.html.

Letter #1 – Lower Interest Rate

Use this template to ask your bank for a lower interest rate.

Your Name
Your Address
Your City
Your Post Code

Today's Date

Bank Name
Bank Address
Bank City
Bank Post Code

To whom it may concern,

Account number: Your Account Number

I have been a credit card holder with your company for the last _____(*number*) years. I would like you to consider giving me a lower interest rate on this account.

It has come to my attention that I am currently paying _____% on my (*name of card*) while many other issuers are charging their customers far less. (*It would be helpful here to list an example or two of what deals other banks are offering.*)

I hope to stay with your bank but if you are not able to offer me a better rate, I will be forced to move to a bank that can offer me better terms.

Thank you for your support in this matter.

Yours sincerely,

Your Signature

Your Name

Letter #2 – Offer Letter

Use this template to make an offer to repay what you can afford.

Before you write this letter let's first take a look at how you prepare the financial statement to include in the letter.

Step 1   - Write down all the headings from your budget

Step 2 - Write down the total that you feel you spend on each heading next to the heading. Use Figure 6, Your Averages Spreadsheet to calculate these figures. Here is an example of a very basic financial statement:

Financial Statement

Income	1580
Council Tax	20
Electricity	40
Gas	40
Water	45
Transport	315
Entertainment	20
Food	200
Medical	30
Debt	120
House	880

Your Name
Your Address
Your City
Your Post Code

Today's Date

Bank Name
Bank Address
Bank City
Bank Post Code

To whom it may concern,

Account number: Your Account Number

I am experiencing financial difficulties because.....................................

Enclosed is a copy of my financial statement from which you will see that after meeting essential expenditure there is (choose one option) (1) only £___ to offer you (or 2) no available income with which I can make you an offer.

If my circumstances improve in the future I will contact you again but in the meantime I would be very grateful if you would also freeze the interest charges.

Yours sincerely,

Your Signature

Your Name

Letter #3 - Reclaim Credit Card Charges

You may have heard of the 2009 Bank Charges test case where the Supreme Court decided that charges could not be assessed for fairness. This case was specifically about Bank Charges and does not apply to credit card and so if you have a lot of bank charges from credit cards, you can try and get them repaid to you. Be firm as some Judges will refer to the Bank Charges test case which does not apply to credit cards – make sure you mention that if they bring up the case. This does not affect your credit rating at all, banks are not allowed to mention this on your credit file.

Step 1 - Make sure you have another bank account if you credit card and bank account are at the same bank as it is possible that the credit card company will close your account after you have made a claim. This is not always the case though, I made a claim with Barclays and they did not close my account after paying out a settlement amount into my account.

Step 2 - Fill in the **Reclaim Credit Card Charges** template that follows. You will need to fill in and send off one letter per credit card.

Your Name
Your Address
Your City
Your Post Code

Today's Date

Credit Card Company Name
Credit Card Company Address
Credit Card Company City
Credit Card Company Post Code

To whom it may concern,

Account number: Your Account Number

I am writing to request that you repay all the late payment fees and/or over limit fees that have been applied to my credit card account.

I do not believe the charges reflect the true cost to your organization and are unfair as stipulated in the Unfair Terms in Consumer Contracts Regulations 1999.

The total charges amount to £_____. Please find a full breakdown of the charges enclosed.

I therefore ask that you repay me the full amount of the above mentioned charges. I have attached a full schedule of the charges and interest with this document.

I look forward to a full response to this letter within 14 days.

Yours sincerely,

Your Signature

Your Name

Letter # 4 - Request to Write Off Debt

Do not use this letter because you are too lazy to sort out your finances, this will teach you absolutely nothing and it won't be long before you end up in the same situation again. This letter is only if you have worked at sorting out your debt for more than a year and simply cannot find a way to get on top of it.

There is no guarantee that your bank will even agree to writing off your debt but it is definitely something worth trying. Have a long, hard think about this first and use it only as a last resort as it may affect your credit file.

Your Name
Your Address
Your City
Your Post Code

Today's Date

Credit Card Company Name
Credit Card Company Address
Credit Card Company City
Credit Card Company Post Code

To whom it may concern,

Account number: Your Account Number

I am sorry that I am unable to keep up my monthly payments to your company. Write your reason here.

I enclose a copy of my financial statement. This shows income and expenses for me and my household. You will see from this information that I am unable to make any offer of payment.

Unfortunately, my circumstances are unlikely to improve in the foreseeable future and I have no assets to sell to help clear my debt. I am therefore asking you to consider writing off my debt as I can see no way of ever repaying it.

If you are unable to agree to this, please explain your reasons.

Thank you for your help and I look forward to hearing from you.

Yours sincerely,

Your Signature

Your Name

Letter #5 - Reclaim Payment Protection Insurance

If you have a concern about how your PPI Policy (Payment Protection Insurance on loans, credit cards, etc) was sold, you don't need to use a Claims Management Company (CMC), you can do it yourself for free. A CMC will charge an upfront fee or take a proportion of any compensation you may be due to you. Your bank will assess your complaint directly in exactly the same way that they treat complaints from a Claims Management Company, so by approaching them direct you will not be disadvantaged.

To download the questionnaire, for guidance notes, for more info and more banks go to www.d7church.co.uk/money.html

Once you have filled in your claim, make a copy for your own records and then post it to your bank. Here are some details for the main banks:

Clydesdale
www.cbonline.co.uk/contact-us/complaints-procedure-contact-us

Halifax
www.halifax.co.uk/helpcentre/ppi-complaints/?pagetabs=1

HSBC
www.hsbc.co.uk/1/2/personal/payment-protection-insurance

Lloyds
www.lloydstsb.com/payment_protection_insurance_complaints.asp

Nationwide
www.nationwide.co.uk/contact_us/making_a_complaint/making_a_complaint.htm

Natwest / RBS
www.natwest.com/global/ppi.ashx

Northern Rock
www.n-ram.co.uk/en/customers/contact-us/internal-complaints.aspx

Step 3 Summary of What To Do Now:

1. Decide for yourself whether you are a credit addict or not. If after reading the symptoms, you feel you *are* an addict then decide immediately to change and break free – stop spending right away!

2. Calculate the interest on your credit purchases using Figure 7

3. Summarise all your debt using Figure 8

4. Start saving on interest right away by using the three suggestions listed.

Step 3 Notes:

Write down in the space below the reasons why you have decided that you don't want to use credit to shop.

……

……

……

……

……

……

……

……

……

……

……

……

……

Step 4 Planning A Budget

The idea behind budgeting is to have control of your money and to do the best you can to stick to the guidelines that you have set up for yourself. The idea is not to beat yourself up all the time, but simply to work towards a more disciplined lifestyle. Each person should develop their own system according to their needs and goals; there isn't one system that works 100% for everyone.

Annual Payments Calculations

The last thing to do before we plan a budget is to work out the average of any annual or quarterly fees that you pay e.g, subscriptions, licenses, etc. Use the following spreadsheet (Figure 9 & 10) to calculate the monthly value of each payment.

Add the full amount into the "Annual /Quarterly Amount" column and then in the "Divide by 12 (or 4)" fill in the number of months that the payment is for then divide by that number to get the monthly amount, i.e. If your insurance is £300 for 12 months then type £300 in the "Annual /Quarterly Amount" column then put 12 in the divide by column as the insurance is for 12 months then divide £300 by 12 and fill in the amount into the "Monthly Amount" column. See the example (Figure 9).

Annual Payments due: To whom	Annual/Quarterly Amount	Divide by 12 or 4	Monthly Amount
Insurance	£300	12	£25
Phone	£45	4	£11.25

Figure 9 – Your Annual Payments Example

Annual Payments due: To whom	Annual/Quarterly Amount	Divide by 12 or 4	Monthly Amount

Figure 10 – Your Annual Payments   Fill in these sheets or download at www. moneymattersbook.co.uk

Preparing Your Budget

Now we have all the information that we need to prepare an accurate budget that will help you stay in control of your money. Fill in the first column of the following spreadsheet (Figure 11 – 'Preparing Your Budget'). Use the guidelines on the right hand side of the spreadsheet.

Record all income here
Record all other income here
Add income and other income and put the total here
Add all your expenses together and put the total here
Subtract your expenses from your income and put the balance here
Record your expenses here

	Current Budget	Adjusted Budget	Final Budget
Income			
Other Income			
Total Income			
Total Expenses			
Balance			
Bills			
Clothes			
Debt			
Education			
Fitness & Leisure			
Food			
Gifts			
Medical			
Other			
Phone			
Rent			
Savings			
Charity			
Travel			

Figure 11 – Preparing Your Budget

Column 1 – Calculating Your Current Budget

1. To calculate your income, other income and all your expenses (except debt) use the averages from Figure 6 – 'Your Averages Spreadsheet'.

2. For the debt column use the total monthly amount of Figure 8 – 'Your Debt Summary'.

3. Take the monthly amounts from Figure 10 - 'Your Annual Payments' spreadsheet and add them into the relevant box. For example, if you have car insurance that is £25 a month in 'Your Annual Payments' spreadsheet then add that amount into your transport box.

4. Once you've completed this column, do the calculations in order to get the balance by adding all income and expenses.

5. To get your balance subtract the expenses from the income. You may have a negative balance; fill it in with a minus before the actual amount, e.g. -£124.

Column 2 – Adjusted Budget

1. Adjust figures in areas that have been included in your three months analyses that aren't "usual" expenses. For example if your car had major repairs and you recorded it under transport then adjust that figure slightly to reflect a more accurate reading. Don't use this as an excuse to change your figures but simply use a little common sense to ensure that the budget is as accurate as possible.

2. Have a look at the most obvious things in the first column that need to be reduced and fill the adjusted figure into the second column.

3. For boxes that you don't want to change write the same figure in the adjusted budget column.

4. Recalculate your balance to make sure that you are not left with a negative figure. (For ideas on cutting costs go to Step 5 – 'Being Creative')

Column 3 – Final Budget

Once you have worked out a budget that you are happy with write it into the 'Final Budget' column.   Transfer the figures from the 'Final Budget' column into the first column of the spreadsheet Figure 12 – 'Your Budget'

	Budget	Jan	Feb	Mar	Apr	May	Jun	Jul	Aug	Sep	Oct	Nov	Dec
Salary													
Other													
Income	£0	£0	£0	£0	£0	£0	£0	£0	£0	£0	£0	£0	£0
Bills													
Clothes													
Debt													
Education													
Fitness													
Food													
Gifts													
Medical													
Other													
Phone													
Rent													
Savings													
Charity													
Travel													
Expenses	£0	£0	£0	£0	£0	£0	£0	£0	£0	£0	£0	£0	£0
Balance	£0	£0	£0	£0	£0	£0	£0	£0	£0	£0	£0	£0	£0

Figure 12 – Your Budget

Fill in these sheets or download at www.moneymattersbook.co.uk

Your Budget

Well done - you've done it!   You have prepared a budget for the next twelve months! The plan from here is to stick to a budget for the rest of your life and stay in control of your money. Review the budget from time to time as your needs change. Only do this when it is essential and not because you are too lazy to stick to your budget. Changes should be made for legitimate reasons, e.g. your baby starts attending school so naturally you will need to increase the education box or you change jobs and your income and travel expenses change.

The idea behind the previous spreadsheet, Figure 12 – 'Your Budget', is that you track your expenses each and every month and don't exceed the amounts in the first column – this column contains your **spending limit** not your spending target! If you find it too difficult to use a single spreadsheet then I suggest you use one spreadsheet for each month and when you have totalled up each column transfer the totals to Figure 12 – 'Your Budget'.

Photocopy or print off from www.d7church.co.uk/money.html the spreadsheets that were used to do your analysis in Step 1 and use one for each month. Your money must be your slave; if it is not, then you are a slave to your money! It can only be one or the other.   If money is your slave then you have to know where it is and what it is doing at all times. I have given you an outline of a few months of the system that I use. You may want to have different headings and adjust it a little, but I find that this works for me because it is very accurate. Just remember, our money must work for us and not us working for our money.

This is a very basic budget, you may want to add or change it in various ways to suit your lifestyle and individual circumstances. If you have not budgeted before, it's a good idea to keep a record of your income and expenses for a three month period and after that add up your heading totals and divide by three to get your averages for those three months. Once you have done this you will be able to start projecting a more accurate budget. Success in budgeting is not having everything perfect, if you strive for that you will be disappointed, but rather do the best you can to stick to the guidelines that you have set up for yourself and accept that you may be out by a few pounds in certain areas from time to time. Don't beat yourself up about it, but simply work towards a more disciplined lifestyle. God wants to mature us so that we can handle the wealth He wants us to have.

As soon as He releases a little bit of money, He is more than likely going to test you to see if you can handle it. There's one thing that will expose people's nature quicker than anything else, and that is money. If we are going to be used by God we must be trustworthy in the area of finances. The first thing that God looks for is trustworthiness, not skill. I have found that there is no right or wrong system. Each person must find out what they are comfortable working with, maybe even develop their own system. The system that I use works for me, as I like to know exactly where every penny is and what it's doing for me.

"No *one can serve two masters. Either he will hate the one and love the other, or he will be devoted to the one and despise the other. You cannot serve both God and Money*."

- Matthew 6:24

Don't be fooled, once Satan has got you in his snare he will not spare you. Keep faithful to God and keep tithing. If you aren't tithing then you can't claim the protection that God promises in Malachi (*and I will rebuke the devourer for you*). You will suddenly find that your medical column has tripled and your transport has doubled. For some strange reason you cannot afford gifts anymore and the phone bill has just shot up. Within a month or two your budget is a mess and you just can't understand what has gone wrong. This is the truth; I have seen it happen over and over again in people's lives. Too many of them unfortunately don't learn but rather live their life in financial bondage. If you think your budget is just fine and you are not tithing just imagine what God would have in store for you if you tithed? Malachi says "test me in this". God has given you permission to test Him; He is waiting for an opportunity to show you His goodness.

Another suggestion that I have is that you should be honest. Work out your budget as accurately as possible, including all possible expenses, even if it means that your expenses exceed your income. (I am not talking about unwise spending, just your needs). Keep a clear written record of all monies in and out and see the great things that God will do for you.

Last but not least, the primary thing that I would like to have imparted to you is the importance of tithing and giving, but I also hope to have given you enough facts to help you realize that you need to get out of debt. God is a God of miracles and we should start trusting Him. If you need a new bed and really can't afford it, first pray about it and allow Him to give you one, or the cash to buy one, before you jump into the world's system. God will always guide you if you let Him and He will show the way in which to trust Him. Managing your finances in the Godly manner can be very rewarding. God is waiting for you to come to Him and to ask for help or guidance. Our God is a loving Father and He cares about the things that matter to us. His heart breaks when His people would rather turn to the world's system than to Him.

God wants us to prosper!

He didn't create us just to survive and live from one payday to the next; He actually wants us to have more than enough. Start out by working out your budget, honestly calculating how much if enough for you, and then trust God for more than enough! I used to live from payday to payday. My life was a thirty-day cycle that revolved around payday. Once I was released from that system, I became as free as a bird. Granted, most of us get paid and it happens every month, I'm not condemning payday, I am merely saying that even the very means that God chose to bless you with - a salary - can be a bondage.

"For we walk by faith, not by sight"

- 2 Corinthians 5:7

Do you realize who He is? He is the great I AM, He is the creator of the universe and He owns all the gold and silver and the cattle on a thousand hills. It's not like He can't afford to prosper us.

Step 4 Summary of What To Do Now:

Work out your annual payments (Figure 10 – Your Annual Payments)

Prepare your budget (Figure 11 – Preparing Your Budget)

Start using your budget (Figure 12 – Your Budget)

Step 4 Notes:

Write down in the space below why you are determined to stick to your budget.

....

....

....

....

....

....

....

....

....

....

Step 5 Being Creative

Ideas for Cutting Expenses

Bills

1. Don't accept the supplier that you are currently using, shop around and find the best possible deal for your bills. Find the best possible price you can get for your gas, electricity, heating, etc. Some good websites are www.uswitch.com and www.moneysavingexpert.com

2. Some utility companies offer a reduced rate on your bill if you pay by direct debit. This not only means that you have the added convenience of having your bill deducted from your bank account automatically (after all, it has to be paid!) but it also means that you save some money by using this method.

3. Another way to save is to see if your utility company offer savings schemes if you pay a fixed regular instalment (e.g. £25 per month). Again this means that you save money and if you pay a regular amount each month you can avoid huge quarterly bills.

4. If you are paying quarterly bills and you struggle to meet the payments it would be advisable to make small, regular payments into your own bank account to save towards the quarterly bill. This way you keep the interest that has accumulated and you have the money needed to pay the bill.

5. If you are the only adult living in a home and are paying council tax you are entitled to a single person discount, this allows twenty five percent discount on your council tax bill. To find out more call the contact number on your council tax bill.

6. If you are on low income, Income Support or some form of benefit and are paying council tax you may also be entitled to council tax benefit. For more information go to www.dwp.gov.uk

Insurance

1. Raise Your Excess

    Your excess is the amount of risk you agree to accept before the insurance company starts paying on a claim. If you have a low excess of £50 to £100, consider raising it to at least £500 to £1,000. You could save up to 25% on your premiums. Insurance is like risk sharing and your excess is telling the insurers how much of the risk you are willing to share.

2. Combine Your Homeowner's and Car Insurance Policies

    Consider buying your homeowner's and car insurance policies from a company that offers both. Most companies offer discounts of 5% to 20% if you buy both types of policies from them. Shop around to ensure the price is lower than buying the two policies from two different companies before making this move. Some insurance companies even offer cash back or other incentives to get you to move to them.

3. Ask for Discounts

    If you don't ask you might not get. Do your research and make sure you're receiving all the discounts for which you're eligible. Discounts exist for having specific alarm systems in your home or smoke detectors. If your car is kept in a garage and not on the street you could also be entitled to a discount. If you are a certain age or have any disabilities you could also quality for a discount.

4. Don't Believe Everything They Tell You

    The insurance person at the end of the phone is a sales person after all and their job is to sell you as much as possible. I can assure you that they are not really concerned about you and your budget. It is very likely that they have sales targets to meet each month and so the pressure to sell is on them which means the pressure is on you to buy. Consider what you actually need to be insured for and say no to the rest. It makes no sense to buy insurance to protect yourself against risks you are unlikely to encounter; for example, flood coverage in an area that is not prone to flooding, overseas travel insurance if you don't travel regularly, etc.

5. Remove Insurance Risks

    Ask your insurance company what you can do to make your home less expensive to insure or check on the internet for ideas. Making simple changes could bring your premium down.

6. Read Your Insurance Policy

    Do you actually know what your policy documents say? There is always small print and all sorts of things that make sure that when you do need to claim, you can't. More often than not it is because most policy holders don't read their policy. If you don't understand it, take as much time as you need on the phone to your insurance company to make them explain it to you until you understand it. Here are some suggested questions:

    -   What exactly does my insurance cover?
    -   If I cause a car accident, what happens and how much will I pay?

- Are there any restrictions on how I or my family members can use my car?

- Do I need separate insurance for business use, etc.?

- Am I protected against accidents caused by uninsured motorists?

- Am I covered immediately?

- Can I insure my property if it is let to tenants?

- Do I need to have proof that I own what I'm insuring?

- Are my fences covered for storm damage?

- Can you cover my son/daughters contents whilst in halls of residents?

There are so many questions you could ask but consider your circumstances and rather ask too many questions than too few. In the past I had an insurance policy for appliance breakdown including things like our boiler. When our boiler did break down, in the middle of winter, they refused to pay for the repairs as our boiler did not have the necessary certificate. We had been paying that policy for years but didn't realise that we had wasted our money. Now we don't have that policy but prefer to save a little extra for any breakdowns or replacements in our home.

7. Keep Your Policy Up To Date

Each time your policy is due for renewal or whenever you have a change in your circumstance, inform your insurance company, as the smallest change could make your policy invalid.

8. Read your Conditions and Coverage sections

Insurers will tuck away all sorts of things in this section. Owning certain animals, a swimming pool or a trampoline can limit or void your policy. Owning any of these can increase your cost of coverage. Read all the small print in your policy as there may be many things that you may not realise, that might void your policy.

Charity

If you give to charities then don't forget to reflect your giving in your annual tax return as it will affect your return.

Clothes

1. Don't have clothing accounts, if you buy on account you are forced to buy at that particular shop and you can lose out that way. If you buy cash or using your debit card, you will get better value for your money because you can shop around, buy at sales, etc. Prices at shops with clothing accounts are usually higher than those that do not offer accounts (even if you pay cash) - this is how the business recoups the cost of anticipated bad debts.

2. Try planning clothing purchases for when there are sales. Put away what you would be paying on a clothing account and use that money only to buy clothes in the sales.

3. When buying a pair of shoes buy rubber soles and put them on your shoes right away to make sure they last longer. You can also put rubber soles on your old shoes to stretch their life a little longer.

4. If your clothes are coming unstitched at the seams, but still look good, sew the seam! It takes very little time to repair clothes and it saves a fortune.

Debt

Apart from the suggestions mentioned previously in ways to pay off debt sooner also consider borrowing money from workplaces that are willing to offer you an interest free loan to pay off your credit cards or other debt with high interest. I am not suggesting borrowing just because you need money! I am merely suggesting that if you are able to, try and find interest free ways to pay off debt that has high interest.

Deductions/Bank Charges

If your bank charges are particularly high, investigate what other banks offer and consider moving banks. Using Internet banking instead of writing out cheques is one way of cutting down on bank charges but first check that your bank's Internet banking is free.

Other deductions could of course be tax. There are many ways to save on tax, have a look at the Inland Revenue website www.inlandrevenue.gov.uk or do some research on the Internet. Consulting a good accountant can often save you heaps of money. A good accountant will advise you and fill in various claims on your behalf and their fee is often only a percentage of the money that they get for you. Rather get some money and give a percentage away to the accountant than get no money at all.

Education

1. If you are studying or are considering taking a course first have a look at what free courses are available from the Job Centre or from other institutions such as Vision2Learn. For more info go to www.vision2learn.com

2. Often you can even receive a grant to study to help with tuition fees - but as always, make sure that it's not a loan but is actually free. Too many people are tricked into study loans that take many years to pay off.

3. Learn Direct can offer you advice and information on free courses as well as help with travel, childcare, equipment and fees. For more info call 0800 101 901 or go to www.learndirect.co.uk

Fitness & Leisure

There are so many ways to have fun and keep fit and they don't all cost an arm and a leg. I can suggest a few things to you, but be creative and find your own ways to have fun and keep fit within your budget.

Keeping fit

1. Walk to work or walk part of the way.

2. Play in the park with your children – this will create a much happier family life and you can be sure that running around after your children for one hour will get you in shape in no time.

3. Take a morning or evening walk as a family and discover your neighbourhood and your family!

4. Gardening which needs to be done anyway is a great way to keep in shape.

5. Yoga and Pilates are forms of exercise that you can do at home with a cheap £5 DVD or find YouTube tutorials for free.

6. Join a community sports team or club, they are often free or only a few pounds. Many tennis courts are available for free in local parks too, get together with some friends and play social tennis from time to time.

Movies

1. Invite a bunch of friends over and have a DVD night - they are a lot more fun and a lot cheaper than going to the cinema. You could even take turns hosting the movie night on a regular basis.

2. Make your own popcorn at home before going to the cinemas; take your own sweets and drinks with you as often the snacks you eat at the cinema cost more than the actual movie ticket. Some cinemas don't allow this so find out first.

3. Use Orange mobile phone offers and go to the movies on Orange Wednesdays (*a current offer at the time of writing this book*) when you can buy one get one free. www.orange.co.uk

4. Use the library - the DVD's are much cheaper and in better condition than most rental places. Also, why not take out a book and read rather than watch a movie – the libraries are full of enjoyable free books to borrow and also has free internet so why not join the library and read for entertainment.

Food/Groceries/Eating Out

1. Have picnics instead of going to expensive restaurants or takeaways

2. Go to restaurants for special occasions not just because you are hungry and don't feel like cooking.

3. Freeze bread if you often find yourself throwing bread away.

4. Buy food on special and store it for when you need it.

5. Steer clear of instant food; it is always less healthy and more expensive.

6. Eat less if you tend to overeat. Most people eat too much; we need a lot less than you realise to survive.

7. Limit treats to one day a week or weekends rather than having deserts, chocolate, crisps, etc whenever you feel like eating them. And it's healthier!

8. Buy in bulk, most of the time it's cheaper to buy for example a 2kg packet of spaghetti than it is to buy a 500g packet.

9. Buy the supermarkets 'own brand' products as they are in most cases just as good but much cheaper than the expensive brand names. Often the supermarkets own brands are actually produced by the expensive brand names especially for the supermarkets.

10. Make a list of what you need for the week/month and stick to it when shopping. It's the daily little trips to the corner shop that will rob you of your money.

11. When shopping, don't walk down the aisles that stock the things that you don't really need. I seldom walk down the crisps and sweets aisle or the aisles that have luxuries that I simply don't need.

12. Don't go shopping on an empty stomach or you will end up buying things you don't need. Have a bite to eat before going to the shops.

13. Prepare a shopping list before hand so that you don't forget to buy anything but also so that you don't buy too much of what you don't need.

14. Have an idea beforehand of how much you want to spend on shopping. It's very helpful to add as you go along, either in your head or using a calculator. This way you won't overspend or get a shock when you get to the till.

Gifts

1. Buy gifts throughout the year, especially when there are sales/specials so that you don't run short of money at Christmas time. Shopping at Christmas time is the most expensive time to shop anyway.

2. Be creative and make gifts for people. Some people appreciate homemade gifts much more than shop bought gifts. The simplest example I can think of is to bake some cookies and wrap them in a pretty box with a ribbon and a personal note. You may have many talents that you can use to make gifts, so be creative. Search the internet for inspiration - there are so many ideas available for free.

3. Don't buy every single person under the sun a gift at Christmas time or for birthdays. Too many people feel guilty if they don't buy EVERYONE a gift, but that is really silly.

   Research by www.swapit.co.uk in December 2010 found that almost 90% of under 18 year olds would be happy to receive fewer presents to help ease financial concerns for their family. Five million people increased their debt in 2009 to buy Christmas presents. In 2010 the average child was due to receive six presents from their family although others may have received up to fourteen gifts from their family.

Medical

1. If you don't have medical insurance put a little money away each month to save for any unforeseen expenses that may crop up.

2. When given a prescription, find out if there is a generic alternative or a cheaper shelf alternative as they are just as effective but cost a lot less.

3. You are entitled to free prescriptions and most medical care if you are pregnant, have a child under one or are on low income. It's worth looking into if you have a lot of medical expenses.

4. If you are a student or on low income you may be able to get help with the cost of prescriptions. You should fill in an AG1 form that can be obtained from your Local Department of Social Security (DSS), your local hospital or doctor. You will get a certificate as a result of filling out the form that needs renewing every six months.

5. Your children are always entitled to free prescriptions.

Phone

1. Shop around, be creative and most of all, read the small print! Some of the special offers that are advertised are not really good deals. For example a package that says only £11.99 for 1000 minutes actually says in the small print "subject to an 18 month contract and £11.99 only available for the first three months thereafter line rental goes up to £29.99". This type of contract ties you in for a very long time at an unnecessarily high line rental. Be very careful when choosing contract phones and take time to read all the terms and conditions – no matter how boring they are to read.

2. For international calls use a service like www.telediscount.co.uk as they are much cheaper than calling cards or dialling directly and much simpler to use.

3. Search for a package that suits your needs, for example if you are at work every day you don't need anytime minutes, so get a package for free evening and weekend minutes, etc.

4. **DON'T** use a landline to call mobiles and premium numbers if can avoid it – always try and use free minutes on mobiles instead of landline calls.

5. If you have a contract for your mobile phone and are entitled to a free phone each time you have to renew your contract then take the free phone every year. You can either sell the old phone or the new phone, but this is one way of making money from your mobile.

6. Most importantly, if you really want to save money, use a pay as you go phone. This way you can control how much you spend on your phone each month and you won't get any nasty surprises when you bill comes.

Mortgage

Did you know that you could save around £19,000 by making one simple adjustment to the way you pay your mortgage? Most people spend at least 25 years paying a mortgage but never realise how much can be saved by making a few simple adjustments.

Here are some ideas that will help you save more than you could ever imagine:

1. Make extra payments, by doing this you can reduce the years that you will be paying your mortgage over as well as save many thousands of pounds.

2. Make extra payments **weekly** or even daily if possible if your mortgage interest is calculated daily. A better alternative would be to switch to a mortgage where the interest is calculated annually.

3. Make extra payments **monthly** if your mortgage interest is calculated monthly.

4. Make extra payments **annually** if your mortgage interest is calculated annually. This way you can take what you would have paid monthly and save it in a high interest savings account and make the payment a few days before the interest is calculated.

Making extra payments weekly or monthly on a mortgage that's interest is calculated annually won't make a difference at all during the year.

5. Make **lump sum** extra payments if your mortgage doesn't charge any penalties for doing so.   If you have savings you may be better off putting them into your mortgage as a lump sum payment.

6. **BEWARE -** Don't make extra payments if you have **other debts** such as credit cards, loans, etc. First pay off the debts with the highest interest rate then start making extra payments into your mortgage

7. Read the small print; beware of **penalties** for early payment, etc.

8. If you have a **fixed low interest rate** for a short period of time you may be better off investing your money in a high interest savings account. When your mortgage returns to the standard rate use your invested money to make a lump sum payment into your mortgage.

9. If you are **near the end of your mortgage** it may not be wise to make extra payments, that money could be better used in other investments.

10. Make your mortgage payment a few days before the interest is calculated. This will give you a great deal of savings without any extra cost to you.

11. Change your mortgage lender.   The lending market is highly competitive and if there are no major penalties incurred with leaving your existing lender then shop around and find a better deal. Another alternative would be to first see what your

existing lender is willing to offer you. Many people don't realise that they can renegotiate their mortgage with their existing lender.

12. Re-mortgaging can be an option if you wish to bring down your monthly repayments or to find a better deal on your mortgage.

Look out for:

- The many fees that can be associated with a re-mortgage. There are fees such as discharge fees, valuation fees, redemption penalties and solicitor's fees.

- Additional insurance that may be required.

- Small print, there is always small print or possibly a catch hidden somewhere.

- Additional benefits such as cash back, discounts and other various incentives that could benefit you.

A mortgage is a huge amount of money; it is well worth doing your homework and seeing how you can make this money work for you. There are new and improved offers coming up all the time as the banks are highly competitive. Make a point of keeping up to date on how to make or save money on your mortgage.

Extra payments savings example

Based on a £60,000 repayment mortgage over 25 years @ 4.59% interest rate with the existing monthly repayments being £336.57

Did you know that if you buy the house used in this example, it would cost you £100,971.58 at the end of your 25 years of payments? If you pay an extra £50 per month towards your repayments it will cost you £91 194.13 and your mortgage would be paid off in 19.7 years instead of 25 years.   Most people can scrape together an extra £50 per month one way or another and the benefits of course would be 5.3 years less repayments and £9,777.45.

Extra Payment Per Month	Total Monthly Payment	Years Saved	Money Saved
£20	£356.57	2.5	£ 4 603.50
£40	£376.57	4.5	£ 8 233.06
£60	£396.57	6.1	£11 176.79
£80	£416.57	7.5	£13 617.15
£100	£436.57	8.7	£15 675.98
£120	£456.57	9.8	£17 438.09
£140	£482	10.7	£18 964.48

Savings

1. For short term savings open a standard savings account available from any bank. Use this to save for things like MOT, TV licence, council tax, a new fridge, school uniforms or anything that you need to save up for.

2. If you are planning for medium to long term, rather shop around for the best deal if you really want to see your money grow. For more information on saving go to *Step 6 Start Saving*

3. If you are pregnant or have a child born on or after 1st September 2002 the government will give you £250 to invest for your child's future. For more information go to www.childtrustfund.gov.uk

Travel

1. If you travel regularly using public transport consider buying a weekly, monthly or annual ticket as it's much cheaper than buying a daily ticket.

   If for some reason you don't need it any longer you may be eligible for a refund. Refunds are usually considered upon written request and surrender of the ticket. These will be paid pro-rata to the cost of the original purchase against number of days of validity left on the ticket at the date the ticket is surrendered.

2. Don't be fooled into thinking that you have to have your car serviced at a branded dealer. A reputable independent dealer does exactly the same work for much less money.

3. If possible use a motorbike or scooter; you can save so much money on tax, maintenance, petrol and travel time.

4. If you're quite good with your hands, learn how to do a self-service – there is so much information available on the Internet and minor mechanical maintenance is easy to learn.

5. Stick to the speed limit, only a few miles over the speed limit can cost you £60. The same goes for parking, don't take chances, as a parking ticket is such a waste of your hard-earned money.

6. Start a car pool for taking the kids to school or take turns driving to work with a colleague.

7. Use your legs or your bicycle to get to work if possible.

8. Your company might be willing to allow you to work from home several days each week, especially if you have children. Negotiate with your workplace to see how you can save time and money on travel.

General Ideas:

Shop around

You can save thousands by doing your homework. Find out who's offering what, who's having a sale, etc.

Ask for a pay rise

Most people don't like asking for a pay rise so they just wait and see if they will get one. Why not ask and see what your boss says, the worst that can happen is that he will say no but imagine if he said yes! For more information on what salary you should ask for go to Pay Finder www.payfinder.co.uk

Use Cash

If you are feeling weak and realise that you may actually blow the budget while you're out on a particular day, leave all your cards at home and take only cash out with you. If you have £20 left in your clothes budget or £20 left in your entertainment budget, etc then take £20 in cash and do something within that £20 budget. It's too easy to blow the budget when you have your credit or debit cards with you. If you only have cash then the decision is already made. You can't go wrong this way.

Hair Cuts

1. Hairdressers are becoming increasingly expensive and if you have a family of four or five on a tight budget, haircuts can take a huge chunk of your money. Why not try cutting your children's hair yourself; there is loads of free advice on the Internet and it is quite fun to do.

2. If your husband or son has very short hair, invest in a pair of hair clippers and cut his hair yourself. A pair of hair clippers will cost you less than one hair cut and they can last forever.

3. Another clever way of treating yourself to a hairdo is to look out for the hairdressers that are training hairdressing students. These hairdressers offer free haircuts, perms, colours, highlights, etc for free if you are willing to be a model for the hairdressing student. They usually take a little longer than a qualified hairdresser would but the quality of what you get is great as they pay more attention to detail and are under the watchful eye of a master hairdresser.

Stop unnecessary spending patterns

Payday Spending

Do you regularly buy something on payday just because you feel you've earned it? Do you really need a new item of clothing or are you just buying it because you have money in the bank? Do you spend an unusual amount of money at the pub simply because it is payday and you have money to spend? Remember your budget on payday and stop payday spending simply for the sake of it.

Sale Shopping

Do you buy things simply because it had a "SALE" sticker on it? The question should always be "Do I need this?" not "How much is it?" Don't be fooled into buying things just because they are on sale. Previously I recommended sale shopping but this was to help you save money on items that you NEED. Sale shopping for the sake of it is unwise.

Guilt Shopping

If you are a working mom or a very busy dad or husband you may feel guilty for not always having time to spend together. Trying to compensate for this by spending money on your wife or children is not the answer. The occasional gift within the budget is acceptable but buying things just because you feel guilty can drag you back into debt. Spend time together; there is nothing that can take the place of a special family moment or treasured time with a loved one.

Mood Shopping

1. Are you a mood shopper? Shopping can sometimes be used as a "pick-me-upper" and of course this is dangerous. The first area of mood shopping is hormonal shopping if you're a woman. There are *those* days when you just need a lift and shopping can sometimes be the cure – or so you think. The problem with this type of shopping is that when you start getting the bills you're worse off than before and could easily slump into a worse downer… and shop even more.

2. Another area of mood shopping is shopping after an argument. You could have argued with your husband, boss, mother-in-law, etc and now feel the *need* to shop. You can also find shopping cheers you up when you feel lonely, if you feel you need a reward for something you've accomplished, if you've received a promotion at

work, etc, etc. The list could go on forever but beware of shopping based on your mood.

3. Eating out is another area of spending that is often used as a "pick-me-upper", you feel grumpy so you take the whole family out to a restaurant. If your budget for eating out is used up then resist the temptation and find something free to do for fun to pick you up again!

Additional Income Ideas:

Child Tax Credit

Nine out of ten families with children are entitled to tax credits and don't even realise it. You may also be entitled to child tax credit so it is worth looking into. The general rule is that to qualify for tax credits you must be aged 16 or over and usually live in the United Kingdom. Child Tax Credit is paid direct to the person who is mainly responsible for caring for the child or children.

Working Tax Credit

You don't need to have children to qualify for working tax credit, if you are employed or self-employed and usually work 16 hours or more a week then you may qualify for working tax credit.

For more information on Child and Working Tax Credits, browse these websites www.taxcredits.inlandrevenue.gov.uk or www.direct.gov.uk or phone 0845 300 3900

Housing Benefit

If you are on low income and are paying rent you may qualify for housing benefit. You do not have to get any other benefits to claim housing benefit. For more information browse this website or phone you local social security office.

www.dwp.gov.uk

Child Benefit

Child benefit is available to anyone bringing up a child under 16 years of age (or under 20 if the child is studying full time), regardless of your personal income or savings. You do not have to be the child's parent to claim this benefit so if you are looking after a child you are entitled to claim. For more information browse this website or phone 0845 302 1444

www.hmrc.gov.uk/childbenefit

There are also benefits for all kinds of other things such as disability, carer allowance, cold weather allowance, etc. If you are really struggling then do some research and get some help until you are on your feet again but don't see benefits as a long term solution. You cannot beat good, honest, hard work.

Too many people choose to rely on the government rather than work hard. The government has fantastic support if you are going through a rough patch and we should be extremely grateful that the UK offers so much.

Child Support (CSA)

Child maintenance is available to you if you are raising children who are living away from one or both of their parents. The money will be collected from the non-resident parent and sent to the person who is caring from the child. For more information browse this website www.csa.gov.uk or phone 0845 713 3133

Get a second job

Second jobs can be a very rewarding way of getting control of your money. Don't overwork and lose sight of what life is all about, but a temporary second job could help you get on your feet again.

Work out exactly how much you need to get ahead financially and set a target and an end date for the job. If you don't manage the second job wisely you could end up trapped in it for life. The most foolish thing you could do is increase your spending because of the extra income – this will only keep you enslaved to your second job.

Rent out a room

If you have a spare room in your home get a tenant (lodger) until you are on your feet again. The government has an excellent scheme in place called the Rent a Room scheme. Under the scheme, you can receive up to £ 4,250 a year tax-free if you rent out a furnished room in a residential property. For more information browse this website www.direct.gov.uk or phone 0845 900 0404

Sell Unwanted Goods

Car Boot Sale

You will be surprised how much you have around your house that you don't want or use that you can sell at a car boot sale. Even if you have exhausted your own unwanted goods you can offer to take other peoples excess or you can browse sites such as Gumtree www.gumtree.com or Freecycle uk.freecycle.org for items being given away.

Amazon

Amazon www.amazon.co.uk is a great place to sell unwanted books, CD's, DVD's, kitchen appliances, electronics, etc. The great thing is that if the item doesn't sell you don't pay any fees.

E-Bay

E-bay www.ebay.co.uk is a great place to sell absolutely anything, just be careful because even if the item doesn't sell you are liable to pay a small fee to eBay. Also, be careful of shopping on eBay, their auctions can become addictive and you can end up buying something for much more than you should.

Step 5 Summary of What To Do Now:

Work out and write down ways in which you can be creative with your spending. Add ideas of your own and experiment with different things. Also, find out if you are entitled to or can earn any additional income.

Step 5 Notes:

Write down in the space below what unnecessary spending patterns you've identified in your life and write what you are going to do to avoid them.

....

....

....

....

....

....

....

Write down any ideas that you have to increase your income.

Step 6 Starting to Save

Saving and Investing

This section will only provide you with a few ideas, if you want professional savings and investment advice then please make an appointment to see an independent financial advisor.

Once you've paid off all your debt take the next step and start saving. Perhaps you have never saved because you are overwhelmed by all the information or because you're not quite sure what to do. I would suggest that you just open a savings account right away and start putting money into it on a regular basis. Even £1 a month will get the good habit of saving going in your life and replace bad habits. It's more than the amount that you save, it is all about developing good habits with your money.

Get a savings account from the bank that you currently bank with and start saving. Once you have started, you will already start to feel better, and once you start seeing your balance grow, you will feel more in control of your finances. Then, when you are ready, start looking around and investigating different accounts and find different ways to grow your savings. When you are ready you can even ask an independent financial advisor how you can invest your savings. Don't avoid saving because you don't know what to do. Go to your bank and tell them that you want to open a savings account and start putting something into it every time you get some money.

If you are more confident and are willing to learn the basics about savings then continue reading this chapter, it only covers the basics but is enough to get you on the path that will take you to greater financial freedom. Once you make saving automatic you won't even have to think about it.

Savings should be broken into three priorities:

1. Building Up an Emergency Fund
2. Replacement Planning
3. Medium to Long Term Savings

1. Building Up an Emergency Fund

This is your first priority. In life you should expect the unexpected, and this is why you need to build up an emergency fund. An emergency can put you back into debt very quickly if you don't have sufficient money to cover an emergency. Redundancy, illness, accidents, car repairs, etc can happen to anyone and when you're in those situations you don't need financial difficulties to add to your already heavy burden.

The emergency fund should consist of at least three months income. Save your money in a high-interest instant access savings account - these accounts do not require any notice to withdraw funds. Start small, it will take time to build up an emergency fund but it will be well worth it. You won't notice the small amount missing from your budget and within time you will be comfortable with increasing your savings amount.

2. Replacement Planning

This type of saving is a way to plan ahead for expensive items that will need replacing in the future. If you have planned well then you will never need to borrow money or pay unnecessary interest on your purchases.

The replacement fund should cover all major household appliances and perhaps even a car if you really want to save on interest. Save your replacement planning money in a high-interest instant access account or an ISA. A cash ISA is simply a tax free savings account in which every UK adult can put £5,340 per tax year. It is just like a normal savings account and you can take cash out whenever you want, the only difference is the interest made in this account isn't taxed.

Replacement planning will help you stay out of debt and always be prepared when you need to buy more expensive items, e.g. Buy a car to last twice the payment period and once the car is paid off, put what you were paying on the car into a savings account. This will mean you will be forever free of a vehicle costing up to 80% more that it's cash price. Now your cash will buy for its full potential and value.

See the replacement planning spreadsheet - Figure 13. This will help you plan your future purchases. Complete this form from any existing debt that you may already have and for any purchases that you may want to make in the future. The replacement date will be determined by how many months you will need to save in order to replace the item. Once in this discipline you will be in a position of buying cash and have what was going to be spent on interest to the lender in your pocket to use in other areas.

Item	Total Cost	Monthly Payment or	Final Payment Date	Replacement date
Washing Machine	350	50		23 June

Figure 13 – Replacement Planning

It will affect the way you use this item because it must last.

It will affect how you care for the item because it must last.

It will help you stay out of debt

3. Medium to Long-term savings

This is where you save once you've achieved your emergency fund savings. Replacement planning savings are likely to be ongoing.

Your medium to long-term savings can be for anything that you would like to save for. A holiday, a deposit for a house, a nest egg, etc. Save your medium to long-term money in an ISA or some form of investment where your money will work and grow for you.

Definitions

Often there are so many 'words' involved with financial planning that we simply don't bother to do any planning because we don't understand all the words used. Here are the basic terms that you will come across and their definitions explained in the simplest possible way.

APR   Annual Percentage Rate

This is the actual amount of interest you will be charged on a loan, credit card or mortgage. This amount is calculated on a yearly basis. The APR will be higher than the monthly interest rate. This is because the APR includes other charges that aren't included in the monthly interest rate. So rather than looking at the monthly interest rate to compare financial products look at the APR to see which product offers the best rate.

Lenders are required by law to show the APR but be careful when comparing, as they don't all use the same fees in their calculation. Always make sure that the APRs you are comparing cover similar fees.

AER   Annual Equivalent Rate

A theoretical rate which shows the rate of interest that is paid and added to the account every year.

EAR   Equivalent Annual Rate

This allows you to compare like with like when looking at different yearly rates offered by lenders.

ISA   Individual Savings Accounts

- ISA's are free of income tax and capital gains tax.

- ISA's have a limit of how much you can save tax-free each year.

- There are two types of ISA's, a 'mini' ISA and a 'maxi' ISA. You can only save in one of these per tax year.

- A mini ISA allows you to save up to £3000 per year tax free

- A maxi ISA allows you to save up to £7000 per year tax free

- Interest credited to the account does not affect the £3000 or £7000 ceiling.

- Money can be withdrawn from an ISA once it's reached the maximum limit but it can't be replaced. E.g. IF after saving £3000 you decide to take out £1000 then you would only be allowed to have the remaining £2000 in that year's tax account. This makes them unsuitable for day-to-day savings.

- An ISA is an Individual Savings Account and therefore cannot be held jointly.

- You can move cash ISA's between banks or companies but first check if there are transfer fees.

- **BEWARE** of small print such as interest rates guarantees that will run out in a few months or penalties for withdrawing interest and even bonus rates that disappear if you want to withdraw your money.

- ISA's let you save in three ways: Cash deposits, stocks and shares and life insurance

Some cash ISA's carry the government CAT standard mark. This stands for Charges, Access and Terms:

Charges - these accounts must have no one off or regular fee.

Access - these accounts must allow you to withdraw cash within 7 days.

Terms - these accounts interest rate must never drop more than 2% below the Bank of England's base rate.

CAT standards signify that a financial product meets certain standards on Charges, Access and Terms. The standards vary according to the product. The fact that a financial product offered by an institution has a CAT mark is not a guarantee of its performance or a recommendation by the government. It simply indicates that it satisfied the objective criteria. Equally the absence of a CAT mark does not mean it should be avoided. Some of the best-performing ISA's do not have CAT marks

Stocks and share ISA's

No initial or exit charge; minimum investment not more than £500 lump sum, or £50 per month; at least 50% invested in EU-quoted stocks

Cash ISAs

No charges; minimum transaction no greater than £10; withdrawals no later than seven days; no penalties; interest rate no lower than 2 per cent below basic bank rates; rises on the back of basic rate increases must occur within one month

Insurance ISA's

Maximum charges of 3 per cent per year; premium no higher than £250 lump sum of £25 monthly; surrender values of at least asset value; after three years, surrender values must be no lower than total premiums

Step 6 Summary of What To Do Now:

Decide how much your emergency fund should be and start saving towards it.

Decide what items in your home will need replacing in the future and write a plan for replacement planning.

Once you've accumulated your emergency fund and replacement planning, set other savings goals.

Step 6 Notes:

Write down in the space below what might cause you not to save. (For example feeling intimidated by all the different options or perhaps lack of discipline).

....

....

....

....

....

Next write down what you are going to do to start saving. If you need more help take what you have written down to a friend or Financial Advisor and do whatever it takes to overcome these areas so that you **will** become a saver.

....

....

....

....

....

....

....

....

Step 7 Training Our Children

"Train up a child in the way he should go, And when he is old he will not depart from it."

- Proverbs 22:6

One last budget suggestion that I would like to add in is that of training up your children. *'Train up'* has the idea of a parent graciously investing in a child whatever wisdom, love, nurture and discipline are needed for him to become fully committed to God. It presupposes the emotional and spiritual maturity of the parent to do so. *'In the way he should go'* is to do the training according to the unique personality, gifts and aspirations of the child. It also means to train the child to avoid whatever natural tendencies he might have that would prevent total commitment to God (example, a weak will, a lack of discipline, a susceptibility to depression).

Hence, the promise is that proper development ensures the child will stay committed to God. All this is great and well, but what does this have to do with finances?

Well, if 80% of Christian Americans (statistic based on a recent survey) are in some kind of financial trouble - and I am sure it is about the same here in the UK - don't you think that it is possible that our children will have the same problems, or worse, to deal with when they grow up? I think that the world has changed so much in the last few decades and is changing so rapidly, that we need to train up our children in basic life skills from a very early age. Unfortunately, this can also cause our children to grow up too fast and that could be just as harmful to our children as not training them.

I would like to suggest that we look at creative and fun ways to train our children in the area of finances. There are many areas and life skills that need to be taught to our children, but let's just deal with finances for now!

I have found that in youth groups, children's church and at home, money can be introduced positively and in a fun way. First of all, have an idea of the basic scriptural principles that you want to teach your children i.e. tithing, saving, debt, etc. Don't be overwhelmed, this can be a very positive experience.

For example, the first opportunity that I had to teach my daughter, Lorah-Kelly, about debt, introduced itself in a very natural way. They were having a "fun day" at school and there were lots of great things to buy as well as all kinds of activities and games that the children could participate in. It was a fundraiser for the school, so all these activities were charged items. Lorah-Kelly got her pocket money ready the night before, and worked out how much she wanted to spend on that day. She was very excited about the big day (she was seven years old at the time.)

When she came home from school and I asked her about her day, she very excitedly explained all the fun that she had and all the games that were played and all the cake and sweets she was able to buy. Then, she piped up and said, "Oh, by the way mommy, Carla and I really wanted to go on a ride again and ran out of money, so we borrowed £2 from Mrs. Heritage. She said it was fine and we could pay her back tomorrow, so please can you give me £2 to give to her?"

Boom – opportunity knocks!

I explained very nicely that it was wrong of her to have borrowed the money. If her money was finished, it was finished. I was able to explain to her about debt and how debt can get you into trouble sometimes and how it's good to practice not getting into debt. Even while she was still young and only working with small amounts of money, I was able to teach her valuable lessons for when she grew older. Naturally, this was a whole new concept to her and we discussed it until she understood what I was saying. I asked her if she agreed with the principle and if she would like to apply that to her life – just not in such grown up words though. She agreed. Unfortunately for her, I didn't agree to give her the £2 to pay her debt; I told her that she would have to find a way to come up with the money herself through doing chores at home or in any way she could think of. It may have been a hard lesson for a little girl, but there were no real consequences for her at that time. Rather now than later when the consequences would have been much greater!

Another idea that you could use to help your children if you like, is a little money book. Once again, Lorah-Kelly can get the full credit for this idea. She has watched me do our budget at home regularly but I was very surprised when I discovered that she too was budgeting. She had a little piece of paper on her desk and it had three columns. At the top of the first one it said, pocket money, the second one said, money spent and the third one said money left over. I was bowled over. I thought this was the most amazing thing since bubble gum. Since then I have given her a little book and encouraged her with her "budget".

She always knew how much money was in her moneybox, to the exact penny. We taught the girls about tithes and offerings and have pretty much left that up to them. We have never given them money to put in the offering pot, but rather taught them the principles and left the decision up to them. If they ever needed help, they knew they could ask. We have had to explain 10% to them more than once. It's a hard concept for a little girl. Please be sure to note that we have always helped the children with their "finances" in a *fun* way.

The last thing you want is to teach your little ones about stress and pressure and all that grown up stuff so early in life. We simply want them to be aware of the principles and hopefully if the principles 'grow up' with them, then managing their first pay cheque will be easy and natural.

There is one last story that I would like to tell; this took place when Lorah-Kelly had her fifth birthday. We had just finished celebrating her birthday with her friends, everyone was going home and we were busy cleaning up the mess.

Lorah suddenly piped up, "Mommy, I want to give Jesus some of my birthday cake, how can I do that?" Whew, what a question. We sat down for a minute and thought about it. I remembered the scripture that says, inasmuch as you did it to one of the least of these My brethren, you did it to Me. (Matthew 25:27) I explained the scripture to her and said that I think that if we put the cake outside our house for a poor person to take, then that could be a way of giving a piece of cake to Jesus. She agreed and very excitedly wrapped up a piece of cake and put it out near the street on a ledge, came back inside and waited. It was so great to see the enthusiasm that she had about giving something to Jesus and it really spoke to me about how we should give to Jesus like that. In South Africa, if you left anything outside your home it would get taken by someone less fortunate. Perhaps in England we need to find a different way of 'giving to Jesus', but the principle still applies – do it to the least and you do it to Jesus himself.

We spent most of the day looking out of the window to see if a poor person would take it and eventually one did come along and she was overjoyed. My children have taught me so much and it is a real honour to be their mother. I want to encourage those of you who have children to start as young as possible with financial guidance. What you sow now into their lives, they and you will reap later on in life and a pattern is developed that they will not depart from.

Conclusion

How awesome is our God! It has been more than ten years since I started writing this book and I can't believe what He has done in my life. My motivation for writing *Money Matters* was because I believed what the Bible says, I believe it above all else. God is always faithful, His word is always true and I have never had any major lack in my life. I don't think I really understood abundance or freedom but after exploring God's word in this area for over ten years I can say that I do now. I have come from praying for my daily bread and seeing God provide each day to praying for bigger things than I never imagined possible – and have received.

"Not that I speak in regard to need, for I have learned in whatever state I am, to be content: I know how to be abased, and I know how to abound. Everywhere and in all things I have learned both to be full and to be hungry, both to abound and to suffer need. I can do all things through Christ who strengthens me."

- Philippians 4:11-13

My whole life has gone from poverty to prosperity and at times back to poverty again, but unlike many poor and many prosperous people out there, I have found financial freedom. Financial freedom is not when you have so much money that you don't have to worry any more, there are many people out there who worry every day of their life and they have more money than most of us could ever imagine. No, financial freedom is knowing that God can provide as much as I can believe Him for. Currently I am believing God for a large amount of money to sow into a project that my local church is working on. Why so much? Well, because God needs someone here on earth to get the money to the church for Him and it would look really suspicious if such a large amount of money just appeared in the church bank account coming from absolutely nowhere! God uses people to fulfil His plans and purposes on this planet and He needs you and I to get this money thing figured out so He can trust us with it so that He can do great and mighty things on this planet through us.

So in a nutshell I have gone from praying to God for £1 for a loaf of bread to feed my family with to praying for tens of thousands of pounds to buy houses, cars, fund missionaries and build my local church. Wow, I serve a great God and so do you! And this is just the beginning…

I know that this book is about finances but the reason that I am even alive today is because of Jesus. My story would never have been written if it wasn't for the amazing work that Jesus has done in my life. If you have never allowed Jesus into your heart, or perhaps like I did, turned your back on Him and walked off on your own path, I would encourage you to give your life back to Him today. Make a clean break from everything that's kept you in bondage up to this moment and hand it all over to Him. Pray this simple prayer from your heart and your life will never be the same again.

Jesus,

I'm sorry that I've tried to do life my way.

I want a fresh start, I want to break away from my past and start over again with you as Lord of my life.

I believe that You died and rose again so that I can be forgiven and free.

Please take my life and make me whole again, I am going to trust You and follow Your ways from today.

In Jesus name

Amen

If you've just prayed that prayer, welcome to the first day of the rest of your life. The best way to grow as a Christian is to find a church and spend time with other Christians, put some time aside every day to read your Bible and pray and before you know it, you too will have an awesome story to tell about what Jesus has done in your life.

If you have prayed this prayer I would love to hear from you. Please get in touch at
 angela@kingsdaughters.co.uk

About Angela

Angela is the mother of four and a pastor at D7 Church, www.d7church.co.uk, author and song writer. Born in Crawley, she spent all of her childhood in South Africa and now lives in Cheltenham with her Brazilian husband, Eric.

Angela has a passion to see people reach their full potential. In particular, she has a heart to see women set free from the lies that the enemy has fed them. She has published many books which covers the issues keeping today's women from being free and she also writes a Blog about what can happen when a woman places her ordinary life into the hands of an extraordinary God! www.kingsdaughters.co.uk

The King's Daughters Conference is an annual UK women's conference hosted by Angela where she continues to explore the theme of being a free woman, as God intended! www.kingsdaughtersconference.co.uk

Other Books *by* Angela

Hope's Journey

"There was a time when all I wanted was to die but now that I have tasted life I really don't want to die until I have truly lived!" Hope's Journey is a heart wrenching account of Angela's struggle with depression & suicide.

Hope's Journey STUDY GUIDE

We all need HOPE. Hope's Journey STUDY GUIDE is about working together to find the hope that we have lost - a practical study to help you find a healthier mental, emotional and physical life for self-study or group studies.

Secure on the Rock

Every little girl wants to know that their daddy thinks they are beautiful! As we grow older that doesn't change we still longs to hear the words, "You are beautiful". But what if your daddy didn't call you beautiful but hurt you and did things he shouldn't?

Secure on the Rock STUDY GUIDE

We have all been through "stuff" that has robbed us of our security - it's time to take back what is rightfully ours. Secure on the Rock STUDY GUIDE is about finding security together ideal for self-study or small group studies.

Passion & Purity

"God made us girls for extravagant, wild, imaginative, adventurous, fantastic loving!" Angela openly shares of how her search for passion ended up in adultery and how she managed to find a way back to purity.

Passion & Purity STUDY GUIDE

Is your marriage lacking 'spark'? Are you good friends but not passionate lovers? Get that spark back and live as God intended you to live - with extravagant, wild, imaginative, adventurous, fantastic loving!

Being a Woman

"What is the true meaning of being a woman?" The heart of a woman screams to be free to love extravagantly and to live intentionally. A refreshing read with lively discussion from six women - it's NOT at all what you might think.

Being a Wife

Being a Wife is a follow on from Being a Woman where we go into the Biblical role of the wife in depth.

Being a Friend

Being a Friend is a part of the Being series and takes a look at how to be a great friend. Using Biblical keys, discover how to have better friendships. Complete with study guide and real discussion with a group of every day ordinary friends.

Being a Mother

Being a Mother is a valuable part of the Being series and takes a look at how to raise our children the Biblical way. In a time where parenting seems more challenging than ever before, Being a Mother offers practical information that can be used in small group study as well as individually.

Esther or Delilah

An honest look at how women use their beauty to seduce men! Whether you like it or not you are using your beauty for something, but are you using it to empower a man or are you using it in a way that leaves him powerless? Esther or Delilah. Which woman are you?

He Restores My Soul

Do you ever feel like you are stuck on a treadmill that is set too fast and you cannot find the stop button? Modern living can often feel just like that at times. Stress, heart attacks, family breakdown and so much more is the result of the way we live our life these days. Press the pause button, take a deep breath, and uncover a much better way to live.

Free

Living life the way it was meant to be. There has to be more to life than this! What am I here for? What is my purpose? Who am I really? I have to find myself! Am I good enough? Who am I? "*Free*" explores all these nagging questions.

Nature's Way

You have the right to know that the government doesn't review the safety of products before they're sold. You have the right to practical solutions to protect yourself and your family from everyday exposures to the chemicals that modern health and beauty products contain. Exercise your rights today and begin taking care of yourself NATURE'S WAY.

The Tale of a Church Planter

The ups, downs, frustrations, joys and everything in-between on the roller coaster ride of church planting. I can honestly say that no recipe or formula for church building exists - God does not work in this way! D7 Church is proof of this. Not because we didn't try, we did try just about everything.

It was only when we gave up and said so to God that we began to have breakthrough. This is our story.

Money Matters

Are you tired of trying to get through each month, living only to make ends meet? Have you read all the books that promise 'seven steps to financial freedom' but lead you nowhere? Or are you someone who has plenty of money but can't find any satisfaction in life?

Money Matters has powerful, yet easy to understand principles that will radically revolutionise your view of money. Money Matters is a set of three books that will completely revolutionise your finances. Starting with simple truths to lead you to financial freedom, followed by a devotional that will assist you in renewing your mind in the area of finances and finally a workbook that offers very practical guidelines along with spreadsheets and tools for calculating your budget.

Money Matters - *Simple Truths Leading to Financial Freedom*

Money Matters Devotional - *Renewing the Mind in the Area of Finances*

Money Matters Workbook - *Sort Out Your Money One Step at a Time*

www.ingramcontent.com/pod-product-compliance
Lightning Source LLC
Chambersburg PA
CBHW081141170526

45165CB00008B/2752